World Book's Learning Ladders

World of Dinosaurs

WORLD
BOOK

www.worldbook.com

World Book, Inc.
180 North LaSalle Street
Suite 900
Chicago, Illinois 60601
USA

For information about other World Book publications, visit our website at **www.worldbook.com** or call
1-800-WORLDBK (967-5325).

For information about sales to schools and libraries, call **1-800-975-3250 (United States);**
1-800-837-5365 (Canada).

2008 revised printing

Library of Congress Cataloging-in-Publication Data

World of dinosaurs.
    p. cm. -- (World Book's learning ladders)
  Summary: "Introduction to dinosaurs using simple
text, question and answer format, illustrations, and
photos. Features include puzzles and games, fun facts,
resource list, and index"--Provided by publisher.
  Includes bibliographical references and index.
  ISBN 978-0-7166-7734-5
  1. Dinosaurs--Juvenile literature.   I. World Book, Inc.
QE861.5.W67 2007
567.9--dc22
             2007019913

World Book's Learning Ladders
ISBN 978-0-7166-7725-3 (set, hc.)

Also available as:
ISBN 978-0-7166-7780-2 (e-book, Learning Hub)
ISBN 978-0-7166-7781-9 (e-book, Spindle)
ISBN 978-0-7166-7782-6 (e-book, EPUB3)
ISBN 978-0-7166-7783-3 (e-book, PDF)

Printed in China by Shenzhen Wing King Tong
Paper Products Co, Ltd., Shenzhen, Guangdong
11th printing May 2017

Staff

Executive Committee
President: Jim O'Rourke
Vice President and Editor in Chief: Paul A. Kobasa
Vice President, Finance: Donald D. Keller
Vice President, Marketing: Jean Lin
Vice President, International Sales: Maksim Rutenberg
Director, Human Resources: Bev Ecker

Editorial
Director, Digital & Print Content Development: Emily Kline
Editor, Digital & Print Content Development: Kendra Muntz
Senior Editor: Shawn Brennan
Senior Editor: Dawn Krajcik
Manager, Indexing Services: David Pofelski
Manager, Contracts & Compliance (Rights & Permissions):
  Loranne K. Shields

Digital
Director, Digital Product Development: Erika Meller
Digital Product Manager: Jonathan Wills

Graphics and Design
Senior Art Director: Tom Evans
Coordinator, Design Development and Production: Brenda B. Tropinski

Manufacturing/Pre-Press
Manufacturing Manager: Anne Fritzinger
Proofreader: Nathalie Strassheim

This edition is an adaptation of the Ladders series published originally
by T&N Children's Publishing, Inc., of Minnetonka, Minnesota.

Photographic credits: Cover: © Jeff Morgan, Alamy Images; p5:
Blickwinkel/Alamy Images; p6: Corbis/Jonathan Blair; p7: Ardea Ltd/
Francois Gohier; p9: Oxford Scientific Films/Stan Osolinski; p14: Ardea
Ltd/Francois Gohier; p15: PA Photos/John Stillwell; p18: Oxford Scientific
Films/E.R. Degginger/AA; p20: Oxford Scientific Films/Breck P. Kent;
p23: Ardea Ltd/Francois Gohier.

Illustrators: Steve Holmes, Francis Lea, Jon Stuart

What's inside?

This book is about dinosaurs, which lived millions of years ago. You can find out what different kinds of dinosaurs ate, how they moved, and how they defended themselves against their enemies.

Diplodocus

Millions of years ago, the world was a warm, wet place. Tall trees, steamy swamps, and thick bushes covered the ground. Huge creatures called dinosaurs roamed the land. The Diplodocus *(duh PLOD uh kuhs)*, shown here, was one of the longest dinosaurs.

It's a fact!

Not all dinosaurs were enormous. A dinosaur called Compsognathus *(komp SOG nuh thuhs)* was about the size of a chicken.

Diplodocus had four sturdy **legs** to hold up its heavy body.

Diplodocus used its **tail** like a whip to swipe at its enemies.

This is a model of a Brachiosaurus (*BRAK ee uh SAWR uhs*), another long-necked giant. Unlike most dinosaurs, its front legs were longer than its back legs.

Diplodocus held its long **neck** out in front of its body.

Diplodocus ate large amounts of cycad, fern, and ginkgo leaves with slender peglike **teeth**.

5

Allosaurus

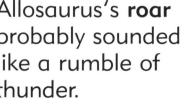

When fierce Allosaurus (*AL uh SAWR uhs*) came charging through the trees, most other dinosaurs ran for their lives. Allosaurus liked to dine on gentle, plant-eating dinosaurs. It had about 70 jagged teeth for eating meat.

Experts find out about dinosaurs by digging up bones. They piece the bones together just like a jigsaw puzzle.

Allosaurus's **roar** probably sounded like a rumble of thunder.

It's a fact!

Allosaurus had an amazing mouth that opened really wide. This beast could snap up small dinosaurs whole!

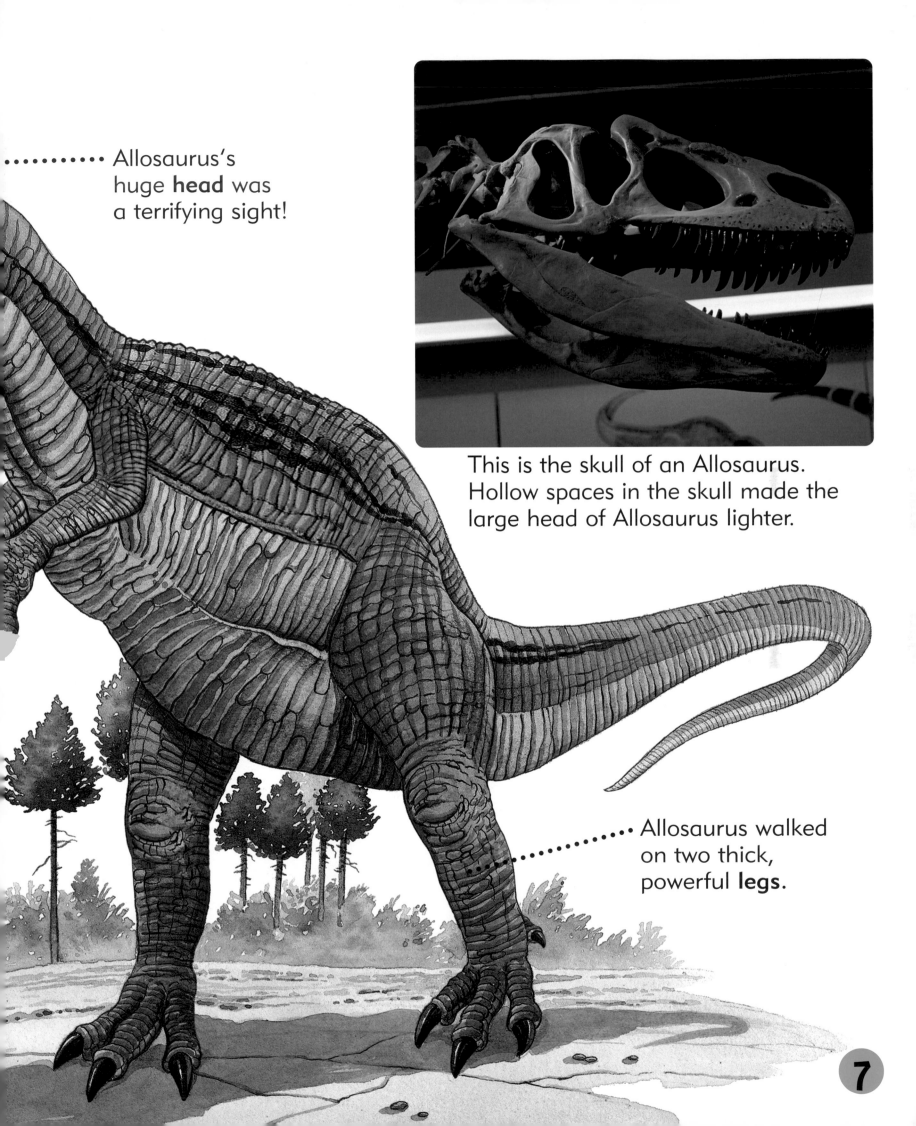

Allosaurus's huge **head** was a terrifying sight!

This is the skull of an Allosaurus. Hollow spaces in the skull made the large head of Allosaurus lighter.

Allosaurus walked on two thick, powerful **legs**.

Stegosaurus

Stegosaurus *(STEHG uh SAWR uhs)* spent most of the day munching leaves and twigs. When it wanted to nibble at taller bushes, it stood up on its long back legs. Special plates grew from Stegosaurus's body. These might have helped control the dinosaur's temperature.

Stegosaurus had to eat lots of leaves to fill its large **belly**!

It's a fact!

The plates on Stegosaurus's back were so big that you could use one as a backrest!

Meat eaters such as Allosaurus ate Stegosaurus for dinner.

No one knows what color dinosaurs were. The designer of this Stegosaurus model gave it yellow stripes. Such stripes might have helped a real Stegosaurus hide in the forest.

Two rows of tall **plates** grew along Stegosaurus's back and tail.

Attackers had to watch out for these sharp **tail spikes**.

Weird creatures

When dinosaurs ruled the land, the sea was full of unusual creatures. Giant animals flew in the sky, on the lookout for something to eat. Let's take a look at some of these amazing beasts!

Ophthalmosaurus *(ahf THAL muh SAWR uhs)* had huge **eyes** that helped it to spot tasty fish in the murky water.

Elasmosaurus *(ee LAZ muh SAWR uhs)* hunted other sea animals. It stretched out its long **neck** to grab food.

Elasmosaurus used its strong **flippers** to paddle through the water.

Fierce Pterodactylus
(*TEHR uh DAK tih luhs*)
soared in the air, flapping
its huge, leathery **wings**.

It's a fact!

When gigantic
Quetzalcoatlus
(*KWEHT zal koh
AT luhs*) opened
its wings to fly, it
was as wide as a
small airplane!

This **strange-looking
fish** is a Coelacanth
(*SEE luh kanth*).
Coelacanths are
still living today!

Dinnertime!

Most of these dinosaurs are munching their leafy dinner. But watch out! Allosaurus is on the hunt for a meaty feast!

Allosaurus

Stegosaurus

Pterodactylus

Diplodocus

Words you know

Here are some words that you learned earlier. Say them out loud, then try to find the things in the picture.

tail	**teeth**	**spikes**
head	**neck**	**plates**

Which giant dinosaur has a long, slender neck?

Which bulky dinosaur has big plates on its back?

Tyrannosaurus

Mighty Tyrannosaurus (*tih ran uh SAWR uhs*) was one of the scariest dinosaurs ever! It would sneak up on its dinner, then pounce. Other dinosaurs had little chance against the Tyrannosaurus's snapping teeth and deadly claws.

An excellent sense of **smell** helped Tyrannosaurus to sniff out food.

These enormous curved **teeth** were as sharp as knives.

This tooth from a Tyrannosaurus is longer than an adult's hand! If it lost a tooth, Tyrannosaurus simply grew a new one.

Tyrannosaurus took huge bites of meat with its strong **jaws**.

You can visit museums to see what Tyrannosaurus looked like close up. Imagine meeting this beast!

Each tiny arm had two **claws** at the end.

It's a fact!

The back foot of Tyrannosaurus was about 3 ½ feet (1 meter) long. That's about as long as a baseball bat!

Ankylosaurus

Ankylosaurus *(ang kuh luh SAWR uhs)* had a clever way of protecting itself. Tough skin and bony spikes covered all of its body except for its belly. No matter how hard they tried, most hungry enemies could not get past this suit of armor.

A knobby **club** at the end of the tail sent enemies flying.

Thick, bumpy **skin** covered Ankylosaurus's large body.

16

Sharp **spikes** kept other dinosaurs from coming too close.

It's a fact!

One kind of dinosaur related to Ankylosaurus had a hard, bony belly. You could jump on it and not make a dent!

Ankylosaurus used its small **mouth** and teeth to munch soft plants.

MaiaSaura

Maiasaura (*mah ee ah SAWR uh*) had a flattened beaklike snout. Its name means "good mother lizard." Maiasaura laid eggs in a nest, as most other dinosaurs did. But unlike some dinosaurs that left their eggs alone to hatch, Maiasaura guarded its eggs and fed its babies.

It's a fact!

The largest dinosaur egg was a little bit larger than a football. It probably came from *Hypselosaurus priscus*.

Experts dug up this egg with a baby dinosaur's bones inside. This is how we know that dinosaurs laid eggs.

A mother Maiasaura dug a cozy **nest** in the sand and laid her eggs inside.

The mother dinosaur brought juicy **plants** to the nest for her babies to eat.

There were as many as 11 large **eggs** in a nest.

This **baby** has just hatched! It looks like its mother, only much smaller.

Velociraptor

Velociraptor *(vuh los uh RAP tuhr)* was a fast runner and an expert hunter. This small dinosaur probably hunted in a group called a pack. Five or six Velociraptors would team up to catch a larger dinosaur.

Strong **jaws** and sharp **teeth** were good for grabbing and tearing prey.

An extra-long **claw** was perfect for slashing other dinosaurs.

Velociraptor raced along at high speed on its two strong back **legs**.

A stiff **tail** helped to keep Velociraptor's body steady.

Velociraptor was covered with feathers.

Velociraptor's large feet left behind deep **footprints** in the mud.

Velociraptor ate small dinosaurs and other animals. Its speed helped it catch its prey.

# Triceratops

Triceratops *(try SEHR uh tops)* was one of the last dinosaurs to roam Earth. This gigantic beast plodded around, looking for tasty plants to eat. It probably gathered with others of its kind in large groups called herds.

A bony neck **frill** made Triceratops look scary.

These three pointed **horns** were useful weapons.

Triceratops sliced up tough leaves and twigs with its sturdy **beak**.

This skeleton of a Triceratops is in a museum. Can you see the big, bony frill behind its head?

Triceratops had stumpy legs with short, fat **toes**.

It's a fact!

Dinosaurs died out millions of years ago. A giant rock from space may have hit Earth, sending up a huge cloud of dust that blocked out the sun. The dinosaurs could not survive.

On the attack

Tyrannosaurus is about to attack with its strong jaws and enormous teeth. Velociraptor is guarding its egg-filled nest.

Tyrannosaurus

Maiasaura

Velociraptor

24

Words you know

Here are some words that you learned earlier. Say them out loud, then try to find the things in the picture.

teeth	nest	eggs
frill	horns	toes

Triceratops

Which dinosaur has a bony frill behind its head?

Did you know?

The name *dinosaur* means *terrible lizard*. But dinosaurs were not lizards. They were closely related to birds. In fact, scientists discovered that the Tyrannosaurus was closely related to the chicken!

People did not even know until the 1800's that dinosaurs had existed.

Scientists once thought that Tyrannosaurus walked slowly and held its body straight up and down, dragging its tail. Today, scientists think the dinosaur ran as fast as 25 miles (40 kilometers) per hour, with its body even to the ground and its tail in the air.

Scientists discover about seven new kinds of dinosaurs every year.

The name *Triceratops* means *three-horned face.*

The name *Stegosaurus* means *roofed lizard.*

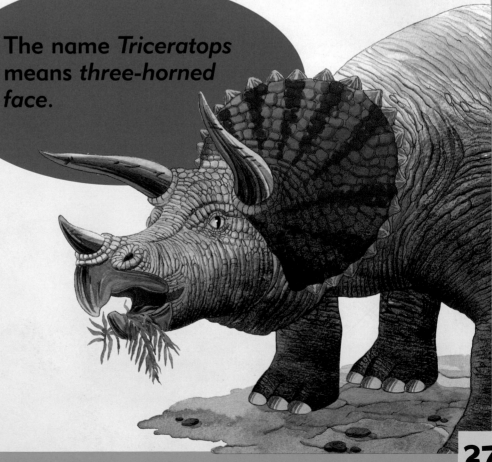

Puzzles

Close-up!

We've zoomed in on parts of dinosaurs that you have seen in this book. Can you figure out whose they are?

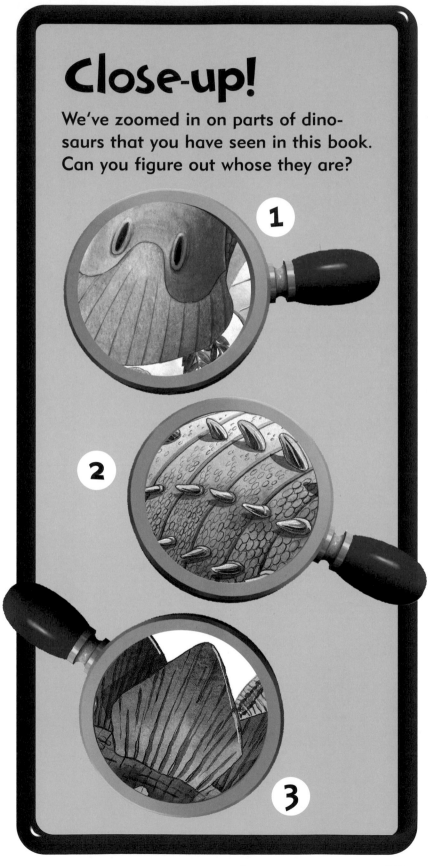

1

2

3

Answers on page 32.

Double trouble!

These two pictures of dinosaurs look the same, but they aren't. Can you find five differences?

a

b

Match up!

Match each word on the left with its picture on the right.

1. Stegosaurus

2. Maiasaura

3. Diplodocus

4. Triceratops

5. Coelacanth

6. Tyrannosaurus

Answers on page 32.

True or false

Can you figure out which dinosaurs are telling the truth? Turn to the page numbers listed to find the answers.

1 Allosaurus used its wide mouth to carry its babies from place to place.
Go to page 6.

3 The creature known as Quetzalcoatlus was as wide as a small airplane.
Go to page 11.

2 Dinosaurs died out hundreds of years ago.
Go to page 23.

4 Velociraptor liked to eat the eggs of other dinosaurs.
Go to page 21.

5 Ankylosaurus had a hard, bony belly.
Go to page 17.

Answers on page 32.

Find out more

Books

Barnum Brown: Dinosaur Hunter, David Sheldon (Walker & Company, 2006)
Meet Barnum Brown, a scientist who discovered many dinosaur fossils in the late 1800's.

Dinosaurs Galore! Giles Andreae (Tiger Tales, 2004)
Rhyming verses teach you about a dozen of the most well-known dinosaurs.

The Day the Dinosaurs Died, Charlotte Lewis Brown (HarperCollins, 2006)
The author explains the asteroid theory, one of the most popular theories about how the dinosaurs died out.

Dinosaur Discoveries, Gail Gibbons (Holiday House, 2005)
Learn how the many discoveries of dinosaurs in the past have brought us to our present knowledge about them.

Dinosaurs, Elaine Landau (Children's Press, 2006) 6 volumes
Each book in this series features one of these groups of dinosaurs: Apatosaurus, Pterosaurs, Stegosaurus, Triceratops, Tyrannosaurus rex, and Velociraptor.

Websites

Dino Directory, Natural History Museum, London
http://internt.nhm.ac.uk/jdsml/nature-online/dino-directory
An A-Z directory of 323 dinosaurs with descriptions and photos of each, plus a guide to body shapes and a dinosaur timeline make this almost a one-stop place for dinosaur fans.

Dinosaur Fun! Jill Dembsky
http://users.tellurian.com/teach/dinosaur/
Choose one of nine dinosaurs and follow the suggested activities to help you get acquainted with it.

KidsDinos, Kids Know It Network
http://www.kidsdinos.com
Discover amazing facts about dinosaurs, use an interactive tool to help you learn their names, and vote for your favorite dinosaur.

Sue at The Field Museum: Just for Kids, The Field Museum, Chicago
http://archive.fieldmuseum.org/sue/#index
If you can't get to Chicago to see Sue, the giant *T. rex*, you can meet her online through photos, flip books, and games designed by the museum staff.

Zoom Dinosaurs, Enchanted Learning
http://www.enchantedlearning.com/subjects/dinosaurs/
This website for students is arranged from very easy to advanced, and includes dinosaur anatomy, fossil discoveries, theories about extinction, classification, and definitions.

Answers

Puzzles
from pages 28 and 29

Close-up!
1. Maiasaura's flat snout
2. Ankylosaurus's spines
3. Stegosaurus's back plates

Double trouble!
In picture b, the volcano has no smoke, there are only three Velociraptors, the Pterodactylus is flying toward the right, the Triceratops in the background is facing left, and there is only one plant in the bottom left corner.

Match up!
1. f   4. a
2. b   5. e
3. d   6. c

True or false
from page 30

1. false   4. false
2. false   5. false
3. true

Index